BUDDHA AND JESUS: CONVERSATIONS reflects
a creative new approach to religious thought.

Our age has seen a meeting of the great religious tra-
ditions. Thomas Merton, toward the end of his life,
found Buddhism more and more illuminating. It did
not take him from Christianity; instead, Buddhism
clarified his own tradition for him, renewing it. Many
people in the West are turning East for answers. At
the same time, people from Eastern religious traditions
find a source of life and hope in the teachings of Jesus.
Gandhi, for example, was inspired by the Sermon on
the Mount.

"From a Christian perspective," Carrin Dunne writes,
"I see Buddha as a precursor, preparing the way of
the Lord. From a Buddhist perspective, I see Jesus as a
true successor of the Buddha."

BUDDHA AND JESUS: CONVERSATIONS consists
of a series of imagined dialogues between Jesus and
Buddha — dialogues which cover everything from
human suffering and sin to the joys which await the
person who is daring enough to be open to the truth.
Written in the spirit of the late Thomas Merton, BUDDHA
AND JESUS: CONVERSATIONS is not a defense of one
religion against another, but rather a conversation between
friends who are involved in the same religious journey.
The dialogues are followed by quotations from Buddhist
and Christian scripture, juxtaposed to show the
similarity between the teaching of Jesus and Buddha,
without ignoring the unique nature of each tradition. This
section of the book serves as an illumination of the
dialogues which precede it. It is also a fruitful source
of meditation in its own right.

Neither Buddha nor Jesus left us any writings. Their
lives and their teachings were recorded by their

followers, and in an important way this process continues in our own time: each person who encounters Buddha or Jesus must come to a personal understanding, an interpretation, just as the original followers did.

So the Buddha and the Jesus of this book are not the Buddha and Jesus of tradition. They are personal re-creations of the author. They speak to the needs and concerns of our age, rather than to the needs and concerns of ancient South Asia or ancient Palestine. Yet all of these needs, ancient and modern, are expressions of the same search, a religious direction which is finally beyond words. This direction is found in the life of Gotama Buddha as well as the life of Jesus Christ.

The differences between Buddhism and Christianity are not ignored here. They also form part of the dialogue. But the differences are finally not the point. They are different aspects of the same search. Here Gotama tells Jesus, "The underlying claim of your way of healing is that forgiveness is unfailing. The underlying claim of my way is that the opportunity of finding enlightenment is unfailing. Both point to an unfailing source of life." And Jesus says, "Gotama emphasizes the preparation of the soil, while I emphasize the gift of the seed. But neither could come to fruition without the other."

The purpose of this book is expressed at the end of the first dialogue. Simon asks Jesus, "Rabbi, do you mean that when we listen to Gotama we should recognize you?" And Jesus answers, "Listen for the voice of the Spirit, for that which enlarges the mind and frees the heart, brings together what was scattered and lost, holds fast in unswerving fidelity, instills peace, comforts and endures.

"Happy are you if you hear that voice!"

BUDDHA AND JESUS:

CONVERSATIONS

CARRIN DUNNE

TEMPLEGATE   Springfield, Illinois

Published by:
Templegate Publishers
P.O. Box 5152
Springfield, IL
62705

ISBN: 0-87243-057-X

Manufactured in the United States of America

INTRODUCTION

What am I trying to do by arranging a meeting between Jesus of Nazareth, the Christ, and Siddhartha Gotama, the Buddha? Have you ever brought together two people both of whom you love dearly but who were previously unknown to one another? You probably had the feeling that were they to meet they would become fast friends, that they would find the same joy in one another that you find in each of them, and that the love which binds you to them separately would soon bind the three in one. Were this to happen it would bring you great happiness because of the new level of sharing and because of the unity it would give to your life.

I stand within the Christian tradition and for some years now I have had a growing interest in Eastern religions, particularly Buddhism. It occurred to me that the time had come to examine these two attractions, to see what they are saying to one another. At a certain level the dialogues are conversations between my inner Jesus and my inner Gotama. I wondered at the outset if one would refute the other, if they would reach a parting of the ways, if they would fuse. What actually happened is that they became friends. While following different ways, which remain different, they found that they are on the same indefinable Way - that great Way which cannot be expressed in words but which is exhibited indirectly from time to time through the interaction of their ways.

One of the most beautiful features of true friendship is that it allows for sharing without loss of individuality. In fact, through the relationship the two personalities are brought out more clearly, more fully than would have been possible had they remained in isolation. I found it happening in my

own soul - what Jesus is for me and what Gotama
is for me has become much clearer and somehow
more interior. They do not fuse, though I must
confess there were moments in the dialogues when
I had to fight the temptation to force that fusion.
There were also moments when I was tempted to
overaccentuate their differences. We are never too
comfortable with polarities though the tension they
generate is the very stuff of life. We are always
tempted to resolve it one way or another, whether
by fusion in which individuality is lost or by
splitting apart in which communion is lost. But it
is between the two poles and in privileged
moments that the Way is glimpsed.

Since I thought of it primarily as an inner
conversation, I was never too concerned about
the anachronisms involved in bringing together
two figures who lived rather far apart in time and
space. Nor did it bother me that sometimes they
betray knowledge of things which happened long
after their respective lifetimes. I figured that they
would know all that I know, if not more. But
there are other ways in which we can look at
their ability to converse. It can be seen as a
conversation between two great traditions person-
ified by their founders. It can be seen as an aspect
of the mysterious communion of saints, which
somehow transcends ordinary human limitations.
Jesus' conversation with Moses and Elijah on the
Mount of the Transfiguration. is of this order. The
connection between the Transfiguration and the
dialogues between Jesus and Gotama is hinted at
in Jesus' conversation with Simon, which can be
seen as a reflection on the methodology underlying the entire book.

Perhaps the reader is wondering at this point
what public value my inner conversations might
have. I propose them as a model for one way

of carrying on the spiritual journey in our times - a journey marked by a quest for individuation on the one hand and for world community on the other. It is also good for us to remember that since neither Jesus nor Gotama left any writings, all that we know of either of them and their ways is what has been filtered through the minds and hearts of those who knew them either in this life or in the spirit. Even in those writings which claim to be the authentic sayings of the Masters, the Gospels and the Sutras, the very selection and arrangement of those sayings represents a discreet intrusion of the compiler. I was well aware of that factor in putting together the juxtapositions which make up the second part of this book. I am not inclined to apologize for the filter, however. I believe that a genuine part of what Jesus is, and what Gotama is, is what they are in human minds and hearts. This may be what St. John had in mind when he said that, if all Jesus said and did were to be written down in books, the whole world could not contain them. What they are in my heart and mind, and in your heart and mind, is part of their fullness. It is also a revelation of who *we* are.

From a larger point of view, conversations such as these between the great Masters of East and West may help more than we realize in the present struggle of mankind. We are living in a period of transition from history to world history, one which may prove as momentous as the earlier transition from prehistory to history. It has not been easy, as is clearly seen by the world wars which have ravaged our century and the cold wars which have paralyzed it. If we look back in time, we see that the only forces able to survive vast cultural changes and destruction of civilizations

7

are the great religions. In an age in which East and West are converging, whether happily or unhappily, perhaps Jesus and Gotama can point the way.

The possibility of fruitful interplay between Christianity and Eastern disciplines was first opened up for me by the later writings of Thomas Merton. At that time I was also doing some work on the role of Socrates in the thought of Soren Kierkegaard. It intrigued me that Socrates, a pagan philosopher, should figure so centrally in the work of an author whose sole aim was to clarify the meaning of Christianity. Kierkegaard saw Socrates as a precursor of Christ, and an indispensable one at that - levelling mountains and filling in valleys in the human personality, destroying paganism and thus preparing men's minds and hearts to receive the Good News. I wondered at the time if the therapy Buddhism proposes, relieving men of their illusions and delusions, is not one of the same order. Thus, from a Christian perspective I see Gotama as a precursor, preparing the way of the Lord. From a Buddhist perspective I see Jesus as a true successor of the Buddha. In the third conversation Gotama gives Jesus the robe and the bowl, symbols of the patriarchate in Zen Buddhism, and in the sixth conversation Gotama refers to Jesus as Maitreya, the Buddha of the future, whose name means "full of kindness." The conversations follow the earthly career of Jesus and tend to become more and more concrete; the juxtapositions follow the development of Gotama and tend to become more and more universal.

Carrin Dunne

CONVERSATIONS

THE FIRST DIALOGUE

I

Simon speaks privately with the Master.

Simon: Rabbi, I must know what happened this morning. I thought I saw two men out there on the water, walking on it and conversing. I saw them twice, then I saw only one, and there was something about him, about the way he carried himself. I thought it was you. Before I knew what I was doing, I found myself calling out to him, and it seemed that he responded and invited me to come. Then I got out of the boat and ran — I am *sure* it really happened — across the water towards him. But all at once I realized what I was doing and sank. The next thing I knew you were pulling me into the boat and the vision was gone. Was I hallucinating or was it really you out there?

Jesus: What does your heart tell you?

Simon: That if I had not been so silly, if my attention had not suddenly been caught up with "Look at me!" I should have reached you there.

Jesus: Is there something different about reaching me there and reaching me here?

Simon: Yes, there is. I don't know how to explain it . . . Certainly I am with you now. No one could doubt that. No one would laugh at me the way they did this morning. And yet it is not the same. I almost want to say that everything is flat and less real now. But that is not really true either. It is just that I feel that had I made it to you this morning, I would have seen your soul face to face the

13

way I see your body now.

I don't know whether I want you to tell me it was real or that it was all a dream. I can hardly believe that something so total, so complete was not real. And having had a taste of that I can hardly bear to wake up and find that there is only this.

Jesus: Simon, you surprise me. That experience seems to have made your ordinary activities insignificant to you. Can it be such a good thing if it empties all the meaning from your daily life, as if the experience alone were important?

Simon: Oh, Rabbi, let me stay there a while longer.

Jesus: No, don't misunderstand me. I don't want to take your experience away from you. On the contrary, you are taking it away from yourself. The gift of ecstasy is not for purposes of contrast, giving a man a taste of the sublime in order to detach him from the mundane. Were it so, it would be better to be spared the gift than to be condemmed by it to permanent disappointment in the drabness of one's daily life. Rather think of the gift as a hint, a clue to what is always there, always at hand, always given. Even now the desire of your heart is within reach.

Simon: Show me how to reach out for it, Rabbi.

Jesus: You already know the way, Simon. What did you do this morning?

Simon: I don't know. It just happened. And just as suddenly it was gone.

Jesus: Then recall how it was lost. It is by letting
            yourself be totally absorbed by *whatever*
            you go through - it does not even have to
            be pleasurable - that paradise is regained. No
            doubt the quiet beauty of the early morning
            predisposed you to the very simple act of
            letting go, and as simply as that you slipped
            past the Angel who blocks the way to para-
            dise with flaming sword. Just as simply you
            returned to yourself and the visit to
            paradise was over.

Simon: But, Rabbi, how can I avoid returning to
            myself?

Jesus: You cannot avoid it. It is a necessary
            rhythm, like the regular beating of the
            human heart, like the inspiration and expi-
            ration of the divine breath. What you can
            learn to avoid is returning too soon, before
            the experience has reached its natural
            completion. It was aborted this morning
            because you have not yet learned to surrender
            mind and heart. You were carried away for
            a few moments but because it was not a
            willing surrender you reacted by running
            back to yourself. We humans have been
            given a high freedom and we hate to let it
            go. What we do not sufficiently realize is
            that by laying it down willingly we are
            able to take it up again transformed.

Simon: Will you show me how to let go willingly?

Jesus: Now you are grief-stricken because you
            lost this morning's experience too soon.
            You would love to recapture an experience
            which is now lost in the past. Meanwhile,
            your longing for that moment is causing

you to lose what is presently at hand, the
gift of being with me now, an opportunity
for which many men will one day envy you,
Simon - though their envy is as misplaced
as your grief. But, if nothing else, you
could enter fully into your present experience of grief. Give yourself over to grief
so completely that there is no longer any
Simon, only grief taking place. Allow the
grief to continue until it spends itself. Then
return to Simon again. In surrendering to
the grief there is release from self, and self,
according to Gotama, is the root of all
pain. Gotama is a master of the art of
surrender; you could learn much from
him, Simon. Gotama is the master of the
art of surrender; but I show also the way of
the return.

Simon: Why should anyone want to return from
the bliss of losing himself? Perhaps to go
forth from yourself without returning is
what death is. If my going forth this
morning is any example, it would mean
that death is unending bliss. Could it be
so, Master?

Jesus: You fail to see the importance of returning. It is only by returning to yourself that
you can make the experience truly your
own through trying to understand it -
something we are now doing together. First
you allow an experience to occur, letting
yourself be led by it wherever it will
take you, and with as little interference
from yourself as possible. When it comes
to its proper end, not cut off before its
time by your intrustion, then you return

16

to yourself. Yet by seeking to understand
what has occurred, you give the experience
an opportunity to continue, not as experience but as meaning, no longer in time
but now in eternity. The meaning of your
grief will stay with you, but not the pain
of the experience. Have you noticed how
you tend to repeat the same mistakes
time and again, until at last you understand
what is happening and why it happens, and
then you are free? The self to which you
return is always a greater self, not only
enhanced by growth in experience but
transformed by growth in understanding.
By the going forth and the return, Gotama
would say that you are being progressively
freed from illusion, while I would say that
you are growing in ever closer resemblance
to your heavenly Father, who is Light,
and in whom there is no darkness at all.

*A few of the companions have drawn near
and overheard the last of the conversation.
Philip speaks up: "Rabbi, show us the
Father and we shall ask no more."*

Jesus: Philip, when you have eyes to see and ears
to hear you will know that that is what
I am always doing. Just now Simon and I
have been speaking of the going forth and
the return through which the human soul
draws near its Source. It has not been given
you to look directly upon the face of the
Father nor to behold directly the wonder
of the human soul. What you are able to
see is that to which you go forth and that
to which you return, and it is by being

17

	watchful and faithful on this sacred journey that you pray in secret to your heavenly Father.
Simon:	Should we take part in synagogue services, Rabbi, if true prayer takes place in secret?
Jesus:	Prayer - public or private - is a sign of the hidden communion, just as my miracles are visible signs of how things really are which remains invisible. Sometimes the signs are empty, a language that has lost its significance, a human appearance without human soul. Sometimes the signs are mistaken for the reality, and when that happens they no longer serve to awaken, but instead mislead and stunt the growth which they were intended to nourish. I suppose this is why Gotama prefers to maintain a holy silence with regard to God and the soul, speaking only what can be clearly spoken.
Philip:	You speak so often of Gotama lately, Master. What has this stranger got to do with us?
Jesus:	Philip, you show by your very words how much you are in need of what he has to give. Ask yourself what it is that prevents you from giving him a hearing. Is it a kind of smugness, an assurance that he has no truth to give you which you have not already received from my lips? Is it fear that he will take you away from me or prove me wrong? Do you have the same hostility towards Moses or Elijah? You have seen me conversing with them as well.

18

Simon: But Moses and Elijah belong to our own tradition, Master. They are fathers of our tradition, and it was a sacred confirmation of what our hearts had told us about you to see you speaking with them, as well as a joyful marriage between the old and the new.

Jesus: You see, your hearts bade you to listen to me long before your minds were able to see the connection between my words and deeds and what you have been taught to believe. Learn to trust the heart. I do not mean that you should ignore the mind's questions, but just as you should open your hearts to an experience, allowing that experience to come to its fullness in your consciousness, so you should open your hearts to great wayfarers who allow their paths to spread out before you. Give voice to your own doubts and hesitations by holding conversation with them. If you truly hear them and they truly hear you, how can there fail to be growth in light? The Spirit which is being given to you is not one to entrench you in a small sectarian world. It is a spirit which overcomes barriers between them, not through destruction of a world's unique character but through communion between worlds. In that communion lies the Way which is beyond all ways.

Simon: Would conversation such as this be another form of prayer, Rabbi?

Jesus: It is not another form but a higher form
          of the same going forth and return. Prayer
          is sometimes described as conversation with
          God. But how can we converse with that
          which is beyond language? We converse
          with humans, with ourselves and others,
          with nothing beyond or beneath language.
          Through this, conversation can lead to a
          freeing of mind and heart, which is God's
          silent word spoken to us. Our unspoken
          response is the quickening which takes
          place within, the leap of joy, the recogni-
          tion, the expansion of our life.

Simon: You speak of a silent word and an unspoken
          response. Is it the same as Gotama's holy
          silence?

Jesus: The meaning of Gotama's silence is mani-
          fold. There is a story which Gotama tells
          about a man who was wounded by a
          poisioned arrow. Before the man would
          permit the arrow to be extracted he
          demanded to know who shot the arrow,
          what kind of arrow was used, and what
          kind of poison. Of course the man died
          before his question could be answered. In
          the same way Gotama teaches that should
          we insist on understanding God and the
          soul before undertaking our therapy, we
          will be dead from our many sicknesses
          long before our minds have attained
          satisfaction.

Philip: Do you agree with him on this point,
          Master?

Jesus: Don't you see that what Gotama warns
          against is the fatal mistake of the Pharisees?

20

I have warned them more than once that
they will die in their sins for refusing to
recognize either John the Baptist or me. I
say "refuse to recognize" for the works of
healing and liberation are there for all to
see, the sure sign by which the Holy Spirit
is recognized. Had their hearts been attuned
to the spirit how could they have failed to
acknowledge me? It is in this same way that
you will recognize whether Gotama is with
me or against me. But because I do not fit
their ideas of God or Messiah, they cannot
accept me. The stubbornness of their minds
renders their hearts stupid. The intelligence
of the heart, which is the highest intelligence of all, is atrophied in them. It is
this danger which Gotama warns against
and seeks to eliminate through his silence.

Simon: But, Rabbi, why is it then that you continue to speak of God and the soul?

Jesus: I respect Gotama's choice. And I often
wonder to what extent my followers will
fall into these very traps. But I am
concerned as well for the dangers involved
in not speaking about God and the soul. It
is, after all, through the Word that my
followers will experience liberation, discover Spirit. The same is true for the
followers of Gotama. Would he be a
teacher if there were no word to communicate?

Simon: But Gotama's word is not about God or
the soul, but about the root of suffering
and the way to bliss.

21

Jesus: Is there then a difference between the Way and the Goal?

Simon: Gotama, you mean, does speak of God and the soul but only in the language of the Way, not in the language of the Goal?

Jesus: When you speak of God or the soul, you speak more than you know. The danger which Gotama sees so clearly is that you may think you understand what you are saying. You may think you have already sighted the goal when in reality you have begun your journey. What you imagine the goal to be may prevent you from ever making the journey, since you are deluded into thinking you have already arrived, and from recognizing the real goal as it unfolds along the way, since it is bound to upset all of your ideas.

Simon: So you believe in silence, Rabbi, just as Gotama does, and Gotama communicates a word just as you do.

Jesus: You remember my story about the sower and the seed? There is a need for good ground - a ground that has been cleared of rocks, thistles and briars, a ground that has been turned and aired - and there is a need for good seed. Gotama emphasizes the preparation of the soil, while I emphasize the gift of the seed. But neither would come to fruition without the other, and both depend on the sun and the rain, the heart's warmth, the gift of spirit.

Simon: Then there is a need for both silence and the word if there is to be any growth of the spirit. You have told us about the

	dangers of the word without silence, Rabbi. Are there also dangers of silence without the word?
Jesus:	The dangers can be even greater because they are more subtle. A good rich soil can be mistaken for an end in itself, but the farmer knows that it is wasteful to let rich land lie fallow, particularly in times of famine. The unspoiled beauty of a virgin is idealized in the human imagination, reminiscent of the lost purity of the race. But what is by far more beautiful and more human is the virgin mother, whose silence is made fruitful by the Word, whose purity is transfused with love, whose emptiness overflows with gift.
Simon:	Then the danger lies in mistaking the preparation for the end?
Jesus:	The preparation is so important, so beneficial in itself that it can seem enough. One can fail to grasp that what is offered is infinitely greater.
Simon:	It is hard for me to imagine a virgin mother. The one seems to rule out the other.
Jesus:	And so it is with silence and the word. How can there be a word which is silent or a silence which speaks? Simon, know that there is a silence which prepares the way for the word and a silence which is the word's highest utterance. It is why I have said that Gotama's silence is manifold. Who better than he knows the art of emptying, of laying low the mountains and filling in the valleys, making a straight path for my coming. But his silence reaches beyond the

23

bounds of readiness. He knows as well the silence of the overflowing word, the pregnant silence of what is beyond utterance, the ineffable groaning of the Spirit.

Philip: I don't mind the idea of Gotama doing some preliminary spadework, preparing hearts and minds for your good news, Master. But I am not easy with the thought of his being on a par with you, of his word or his silence having all the reach of yours.

Jesus: Would you then put limits on the Father's love? Would you have Him refuse himself to countless generations and races of men who have sought Him so earnestly? Certainly it is true that I bring to you and to all men His almighty Word, but do you recognize me only here and only now, Philip? Have I been so long with you and you still do not know me except in this one limited form?

Simon: Do you mean, Rabbi, that when we listen to Gotama we should be able to recognize you?

Jesus: Listen for the voice of the Spirit, for that which enlarges the mind, frees the heart, brings together what was scattered and lost, holds fast in unswerving fidelity, instills peace, renews confidence, comforts and endures. Happy are you if you hear that voice!

THE SECOND DIALOGUE

II

It is evening in Capernaum. The cures
which Jesus has worked among them have
filled the crowd with wonder and excite-
ment. A group of Pharisees surrounds Jesus,
asking angry questions. After a few words
Jesus ends the conversation abruptly and
walks away from the crowd. Gotama waits
for him at the edge of the village.

Jesus: Gotama, I wish I had known you were here.
I have had a hard time of it with the
Pharisees.

Gotama: If I were you, I would be even more worried
about the reaction of the crowd. But it is
true that the Pharisees are at fault. What
they fail to see is the goodness of your
heart; it is only your mind that is misguided.
I don't mean to be harsh, but you felt the
pulse of that crowd tonight. Their eyes were
glazed with enthusiasm, their brains fevered.
Don't you see the mistake? What lasting
good can you hope to achieve with these
bodily cures? Would you have them believe that all their aches and pains will be
wafted away miraculously, their twisted
limbs straightened, idiots made whole, the
ravages of cancer suddenly reversed, the
dead brought back to life?

Jesus: But, Gotama, are you implying that none of
this is possible, that the miracle cannot
happen? How then did life itself first appear,
or thought, or love? For myself, I find
life full of surprises, of unexpected gifts
and guests. Why should we presume to call
all the plays in advance? I prefer to meet
my life with a child's holiday expectation;

27

that expectation provides the space in
which the miracle may happen.

Gotama: It is an entrancing view, I admit . . . but I
believe you create more problems than you
solve. So you perform a few symbolic cures,
you raise the people's hopes to hitherto
undreamt of heights. Then what happens to
the many millions of sufferers for whom
there is no holiday? What do you say to
those hundreds of thousands carried off
by epidemic, famine, war, and genocide?
What do you say to the invalids who don't
get well, the alcoholics or drug addicts
whose lives remain out of control, the
hopelessly insane, the starved, the lonely,
the forgotten? What about your own
countrymen who will die by millions in
concentration camps and burning ghettoes?
And what about death itself, the common
lot of all? Will these millions and hundreds
of millions conclude that for them there
was no surprise, no gift forthcoming? Are
you not preparing for the deluded masses
a cup of bitterness, a cruel and angry fate?

Jesus: Expectations can lead to bitterness, but
hope cannot. If the child has already
fashioned in his imagination the holiday
gift he will receive, if he has already imagined the look and feel and smell and taste
of it, then regardless of what he finds he
will be disappointed if it is not just that.
He will scarcely pay attention to what he
sees, his eyes moving here and there
restlessly, seeking the one beloved object.
Perhaps what he seeks really *is* there, and
is more marvelous than his childish heart

could imagine: will he recognize it if his
hopes are set? It is when our hopes are set
that they fail us - somehow the hope is
always too small. But true hope yearns
towards what eye has not seen, nor ear
heard, nor heart fathomed. It cannot
disappoint. It seems to me that a man
could do worse than face life with too
much hope, if his hope is true . . . that is,
if it is open towards the infinite.

Gotama: Now I understand why my own heart
reassured me about you even when your
actions seemed to compound the delusions
in which the masses are trapped. At first
I was troubled and almost left, fearing you
were merely another charlatan, another
false prophet exploiting the people's
stupidity. You know, I have forbidden my
disciples to perform miracles, nor do I
indulge in such myself. The desire for
magical powers stems from greed and
vanity. Many make themselves rich with
these physical and psychological tricks. In
so doing they destroy ever more effectively
their chances for becoming truly rich.
Worse still are those whose vanity is fed by
the sight of huge crowds lost in amazement,
the thunder of their applause like the sound
of cattle stampeding. These end by believing their own tricks, so great is their need
of believing in themselves. The greedy
swell like huge spiders fattened from the
corpses of those trapped in their nets. The
vain cannot be compared to living creatures,
not even to one as loathsome as a spider
full of poison. The vain are like giant
balloons, sailing high and free, drifting

farther and farther above the earth, smooth and round with no aperture where truth may enter, but vulnerable to the least malicious sting.

It was hard for me to believe that you might be one of these, seeing you so full of kindness. Then when I saw you slipping away from the crowd, hiding in the hills when they wanted to make you king, I was somewhat reassured. When I heard you forbidding them to speak of these things or to mention them in connection with your name, when I heard your insistence on attributing the miracle to their faith - I would call it "suggestibility" - rather than to your power, I was sufficiently heartened to approach you after all.

Jesus: Something you said has troubled me. The faith which works miracles does require an unbounded mind - not the abandonment of critical powers, but the gradual blossoming of a mind which learns to dwell in a welcoming heart. The lowering of consciousness you speak of is only a cheap substitute, a false version of faith. Credulity can be had in a moment: but the mind must learn in patience and sometimes in tears to find its way. And a heavy price is paid for credulity. For it, the mind must be sacrificed, while faith celebrates the wedding of mind and heart, and looks forward in joy to their fair offspring.

Gotama: I see . . . I too have followed a path with heart, a path on which the mind serves a

30

long apprenticeship, learning all of the modes,
tones, ranges and dimensions of suffering,
finally blossoming in compassion. I believe
I am beginning to understand you better.
Yet it seems to me that your methods are
doomed to failure. When you multiplied
the loaves and they tried to make you king
you had to escape to the hills to prevent
them. The incident alone should have
warned you sufficiently of the unsoundness
of your methods. How can they help but
misunderstand when the teachings you
give are so concrete? Instead of lifting
their minds from the gross material level
to that of spiritual realities, you emphasize
the material signs. They only grasped that
you could make much food where previously there had been too little. Immediately
they had visions of a booming economy,
plentiful supplies, low prices, luxuries
available for all, no more scrimping, no
more doing without, no more debts. Instead
of purifying their desires you inflame them.
Instead of gently but firmly detaching them
from worldly expectations you encourage
them. What will it mean, one good evening
on the hillside where they ate to their
heart's content, where they dreamed of
their worries dissolving, when they wake
up and find it cannot go on like that
forever? Did you do them any real service
by catering to their desires even for that
short moment?

Jesus: It worries me that they persist in misreading
the signs. But I know of no more beautiful
language than the flesh. Bread to strengthen
man's body, wine to intoxicate his soul,

that is what the Kingdom is. It is like scales falling away from the eyes of a blind man, like one crippled from birth suddenly dropping his crutches to run free into the wind, like hearing music ring out clearly where before there had been only muted, distant and indistinguishable sounds. Imagine release from anxiety and guilt, a sense of well-being, laughter and love. I cannot tell this good news in the dead language of philosophy; it is only in the flesh that it speaks.

Gotama: You are still a young man, full of passion and the love of life. Basically, that is your only fault. With time you will come to see that the flesh and all its fruits, its joys and its sorrows, are passing. The strongest body will fall into decay, the most exalted soul will grow tired. Nor can the eyes have their fill of sights, the ears of music. There is no laughter that does not breed sorrow, no love without hate. Your great heart is moved to pity for their plight; you would awaken them to joy. I too am moved with infinite compassion for their suffering, but I can show you a way to heal them permanently from their sorrows, a remedy without side-effects. As I have said before, your heart is sublime but your mind is misguided. You do not see that by opening them to hope you keep them permanently stretched on the rack of this world, sensitized to its every ebb and flow. You do not even permit them the protective clothing spun from their grief. You would have them walk out naked and trusting like well-loved children.

32

Jesus: But that is what they are! Only they do
           not know it. They think themselves
           abandoned, left to their own devices . . .
           and therefore they devise and connive,
           scheme and rob to insure their threatened
           survival. They think themselves unloved
           and unlovable, ugly and unclean . . . and
           therefore they cannot love, cannot bear
           beauty, feel more comfortable with ugliness,
           with the tawdry and cheap. How can I
           break this spell? What mirror can I hold up
           before them so that they will recognize
           the marvel that shines in their faces?

Gotama: Can you hold up a mirror that shines
           without an image? No, I see that you do not
           understand. It is too soon for that. But let
           me tell you of another way of healing, one
           less fraught with danger. Once a poor woman
           came to me distraught with grief, carrying
           her dead baby son. She asked me for med-
           icine to cure the child. I did not simply
           point out to her that the boy was dead and
           beyond remedy. Nor did I shake my head
           and mutter, "she is crazy," as did her
           friends and neighbors. I asked her to bring
           me a handful of mustardseed from a house
           where no one had lost child, husband, parent,
           or friend. The woman was overjoyed and
           went in haste to fulfill my request. She
           went from door to door but none fit the
           requirement. Finally, when it had become
           too late and too dark to continue her
           search, she realized and understood that
           death and sorrow are the common lot of all.
           She returned to me at peace. You see, to
           obtain true healing we must first understand

33

that the human condition is one of inevitable suffering, until the cause of suffering is discovered and extinguished. It was her desire that her child should regain his life that drove her distraught from piller to post searching for a medicine. When finally she understood that the desire itself was unrealistic, she was able to let go of that desire and find peace in its stead. It seems to me that you would do a far greater service to the poor, the lame, the blind, the deafmutes, the mourners, the downtrodden, all those crowds who flock around you, if you would teach them how to understand and in a sense overcome their fate.

Jesus: There is a nobility and a strange power about what you propose.

Gotama: If I know you, you would have restored the child to life. The woman would have departed not in peace but in joy. Now joy seems a higher boon than peace, and your healing seems inspired by a greater love. But is that really so? I say that you have not truly healed her but have merely postponed her sorrow which will return in manifold ways and finally in the one dread way, the inevitable loss of her child either through his death or hers. You offer the anesthetic which the drunk seeks from his bottles: there he finds momentary relief, but the real problems remain and grow. You treat only the symptoms of the disease, not the disease itself. You do worse - by encouraging the woman's hope that all sorrow will finally resolve in joy, all pain in unqualified pleasure, you lead her into deeper ignorance.

You solidify her ignorance rendering it invulnerable to the liberating light of truth.

The healing I offer appears lacking in tenderness and true care for the woman's distress, particularly since I could have relieved it in your manner - I too mastered the powers in my youth. Why then did I refuse her anguished cry? Let me make another comparison. Suppose a woman with a condition which requires an immediate operation comes to a physician and begs him for a pill to take away the pain. A good physician will ignore her plea for a sedative and will instead rush her to surgery. The remedy I offer goes right to the root of her trouble. It heals so completely that not only will this particular pain not return but all of her woes are simultaneously relieved. So you see, what appears less loving is in fact much more so. It is not the food I offer more lasting than bread and wine?

Jesus: More lasting perhaps, but is it more nourishing? I am uneasy about extinguishing human passion. Won't life lose all its color and much of its meaning if it is not fired by a great passion? I think I am not yet ready to exchange adventure for serenity.

Gotama: Ah, so that is what you fear. But don't you see that desire can prevent you from appreciating and enjoying the present moment, in the same way that fixed expectations get in the way of what you call hope? Desire is always directed towards a time other than the present. It is anxious for the future, or it regrets the past. It has the effect of blotting out the value of that which alone is

35

real, the present, in favor of that which has ceased to be, never was, is yet to be, or will never be. So you see, my desirelessness and your hope are perhaps not so very different after all.

Jesus: Still, I am not sure that what we are aiming at is the same. I understand what you mean about desire interfering with the gift of the present moment, but I don't agree that only the present moment is real, or rather that only the moment is present. A man carries the burden of his past, not only in memory as something that once was real and at work in his life, but as something that has formed all that he is and is able to be now. A man is no less affected in his present life by what he may hope from the future, whether it opens full of promise or closes in numb despair. It seems to me that looking backward to the past and forward to the future is part of what it means to be human. Does not your way of desirelessness close off these human capabilities?

Gotama: Now *you* are the one who would keep men bound. I have shown you a way of freeing them both from the domination of the past and the future, freeing them to be fully alive here now, new creatures. Nevertheless, it is not my intention to make little of memory and anticipation. They are genuine and important human activities. What I wish to do is free a man from fixation on the past or future. It is one thing to remember deliberately, it is another to be unable to forget. It is one thing to project future possibilities, it is another to behave as

36

though possibilities are already foregone conclusions. I would not have men return to the animal state, mute and content. On the contrary, I want them to become so conscious that they see through the delusions of their own making.

Jesus: But are you not denying the reality of past and future? For you the delusion is to behave as though the past and the future were present. When one can let go of their reality, one can simultaneously let go of their burden. It is true that by following your way a man is relieved of guilt and anxiety - but only by forfeiting his future and his past. Is it not a forfeit of his very self? Following my way a man's burden is not taken away but made light through the forgiveness of sin. Instead of negating the burden and his very self along with it, he is enabled to carry it.

Gotama: You have touched upon my most serious reservation about your way of healing, more serious even that your misleading methods. Why must you introduce the notion of sin? I realize it is a legacy from your Jewish background but I would have thought your first effort would be to dispel that unnecessary addition to human woe. Is it not enough that men are weighed down by guilt without making it even more powerful by naming it sin? Is it not enough that men are paralyzed by anxiety over their uncertain future without tormenting them with the possibility of eternal damnation? Surely humankind is sick enough without being driven mad!

Jesus: A boil must be allowed to fester before it can be lanced; fever must reach a climax before it breaks. But you are wrong if you think that the accusation of sin makes the difficulties of the human condition more difficult still. Strange as it may seem, it alone makes them bearable. Most men simply refuse to face the significance of their deeds. Those few courageous ones who dare to call things by their proper names are sorely inclined to self-destruction, the truth being too horrible to bear. Think of the wretched Oedipus, gouging out his eyes. Man appears to be caught on the horns of a dilemma. Either he flies in the face of reality, thereby becoming himself unreal, or he is destroyed by the reality he turns to meet. But facing the enormity of his deeds, calling it sin, he is able for the first time to utter its terrible name, then to acknowledge that the burden is truly his, finally to shoulder the burden, carrying it with him always. If he carries his burden faithfully without mislaying it in a fit of absentmindedness, it will itself free him from illusion and delusion, causing him always to remember who he is and who he is not. Think how different the world would be were nations to assume their burdens! It has been the greatness of my people, Israel, to recall its past and with the prophets' prodding to recall it truthfully. It will remain forever the mark by which the true Israel is recognized.

But above all, and here is the marvel, it is by the confession of sin that a man is truly and finally freed from the terror of truth so

that he will no longer be forced to flee or
take his stand and be destroyed. And how is
that? It is because sin is only seen and
acknowledged in the experience of forgiveness. Prior to the awareness of sin is the awareness of forgiveness. Whatever dread name a
man may have dared to give his deed, it is
only in that moment of release, of unbounded
and unbinding love, that he recognizes the
full significance of what he has done or
failed to do. And that recognition, instead
of dealing the deathblow, liberates him for
new life. Sin forgiven is a burden made
light, so light that the man carrying it is
more carefree than man without a burden.
He is not only free but freeing. Dwelling in
the experience of having been forgiven, how
can he fail to forgive men their debts? Freed
himself from heaviness and remorse, how
can he hold other men bound? Having
known a gratuitous and unconditional
love, how can he fail to communicate it?

Gotama: There is very little I can say in response to
your words. Truly, if what you say were
true, the world would indeed be transformed.
In some ways your path is richer than mine,
it has greater heights and depths. It is more
inclusive, stretching horizontally as well as
vertically, like the cross, affirming time as
well as eternity. The advantage of my way
is that it is less precarious and more econo-
mical, yet it arrives at the same essential
freedom of spirit. Your way relies on an
experience with which a man must be gifted;
he cannot find it for himself, it must be
brought to him by another. My way relies

on an experience which is available to each man through his own efforts alone. Your way requires a God and men sent from God. It seems very chancy. Even if my message were lost and my name forgotten, it could be recovered in all its purity through the efforts of some future Buddha. Your way requires that the experience be kept alive in men's hearts and transmitted. What of those whom they fail to reach?

Jesus: But what of those for whom your message is too sophisticated? The little, crippled ones who could never understand that existence is pain, that pain is due to craving, that craving can be extinguished by following the middle way? They are the very ones who most readily respond to my teaching.

Gotama: Through their suffering the crippled ones work out the evil consequences of former existences and merit rebirth in a condition in which they may understand and respond to my words.

Jesus: It seems then that my path is not alone in being precarious. Just as mine requires the transmission of forgiveness, so yours requires reincarnation if it is to be real for all people.

Gotama: So we are even on that score. But I wonder if we are not making a mistake sparring like this. I admit I started it by claiming to have a better way of healing. What I see now is a likeness which is perhaps far more important than all the differences.

Jesus: What is that, Gotama?

Gotama: The underlying claim of your way of healing is that the gift of love, or as you call it, for-

40

giveness, is unfailing; the underlying claim of my way of healing is that the opportunity of finding enlightenment is unfailing. Both point to an unfailing source of life.

Jesus: Perhaps our argument has been to the point if it has brought us to this.

Gotama: It is the point at which our quite different paths touch - where the human spirit is liberated from its bondage whether it be through the experience of being forgiven and forgiving or through the experience of universal compassion, that point which is no longer a standpoint, that place which is nowhere and everywhere.

Jesus: The Spirit moves where it wills and cannot be confined, not by you or by me or by both of us together. Let it be enough for us to recognize it when we can, and to know that where we are not against one another, there we are together.

Gotama: So my heart did not deceive me about you after all. On this I think we are in perfect agreement. Dawn approaches and I shall leave you now, though I know that we shall meet again. I think our paths are destined to cross, perhaps to come together, time and again.

THE THIRD DIALOGUE

III

*The crowds move away from the foot of
Mt. Tabor. The strength and strange author-
ity of Jesus' words and the power of his
presence have brought them here. But many
are disturbed: Jesus' language is puzzling,
paradoxical. As the crowds leave him Jesus
knows how strange the Kingdom of God
must sound to them. He walks down the
mountain slope to meet Gotama.*

Jesus: It is good to find you here today - now I
know that at least one person has understood what I have been trying to say.

Gotama: I don't know if I heard it all. Your opening
declaration filled all my mind and is still
resounding there.

Jesus: How happy are they who know that they
are poor, for theirs is the kingdom of Heaven!

Gotama: Who would you say is the poorest of man?
Is it the rich man who worries away his
life in the pursuit of prestige and power,
who can afford travel and dancing-girls
to ease his many tensions, but who com-
pounds his tension by worrying about
what happens to business during his
absence?

Jesus: A poor man indeed, but not the poorest.
What do you think of the man who struggles quietly but fiercely, not to be in the
public eye but to hold the real reins of
power? For him it hardly matters that his
struggles go unrewarded in terms of money
and of fame. He has the secret satisfaction
of the shrewd deal, of shaping history,

45

controlling lives. His is the satisfaction of
carrying weight with the motions of his
mind.

Gotama: Indeed he is heavy, but not with the heavy
belly of a Buddha. Indeed is poorer than
our harassed businessman, but not yet the
poorest: what about the man of science, the
learned philosopher? His is a wealth not so
prone to the swing of fortune, the bitter
quirk of circumstance, the relentless advance
of age. His is the inner wealth of a head
crammed full of the latest facts, the intri-
cacies of theory, the precision of concepts.
Does he not suffer cruelly from constipation
of the brain and frequent attacks of gas?

Jesus: Ah, the world becomes poorer and poorer.
So much energy spun off, so much compe-
tition, such haste, such pressure. Why,
this poor man must be emaciated from all
his strenuous labors, but not yet the poorest.
What do you think of the man who in the
secret of his heart spurns pleasure, despises
fame, relinquishes power, forsakes knowledge, and hones his will to a burning point
in pursuit of spiritual perfection? Isn't he
the most pitiable of men, who has lost this
world as well as the other?

Gotama: And when he finds that there is no spiritual
perfection, what will the poor fool do then?
You *have* found the poorest of men - the
one who would congratulate himself on his
poverty, hugging it to his thin ribs, hoping
to buy with it a higher bliss.

Jesus: And to think it was free all along.

46

Gotama: Fortunately there are few of these poorest of the poor. Strange too how every one of these poor people clutch at their poverty and will not be rid of it, prizing it higher than all the fabled riches of the past.

Jesus: Prizing it even more than the riches we have to offer.

Gotama: They squirm away from the spaciousness of your kingdom or the vistas of my broad Buddha-lands, as though it were exile, or a tour in the salt mines we offered.

Jesus: You must admit it is a strange looking-glass sort of world we propose.

Gotama: Not really as strange as theirs . . . . .

Jesus: This is plain for any child to see.

Gotama: And how does a man come into a share of your kingdom?

Jesus: If he arrives with a large moving-van full of furniture, he will find it very difficult to get through the gate.

Gotama: And if he is concerned about the speed and power of the vehicle, he may pass up my raft.

Jesus: I make it a practice of turning away every-one who has bought advance tickets.

Gotama: And I cancel the performance at the last moment.

Jesus: Parents aren't admitted except in the company of their children.

Gotama: We aim at a mental age of minus one.

Jesus: A play you cannot miss!

Gotama: A play you cannot find!

Jesus: Who can hear it, who can see it?

Gotama: Anyone who is not there and not looking.

Jesus: They will weep for joy, they will celebrate their sorrow.

Gotama: Everyone will envy them their loss.

Jesus: The price of the ticket is your life.

Jesus: And how would you describe the kingdom of heaven?

Gotama: Once I was asked by the crowds to discourse on the very heart of nirvana, the highest stage of enlightment. I agreed to do it! Do you know what I gave them? I stood before them and silently twirled a flower in my fingers.

Jesus: And did they understand?

Gotama: One old man's face lit up with a smile.

Jesus: Ah!

Gotama: And you, how do you describe it?

Jesus: I begin with exciting images like new wine and a wedding-feast. Who would not wish to be part of such a kingdom? Until they discover that they will sit at the table with all the riffraff from the streets, for whom are reserved the choicest places, and that the wine they will drink is my blood.

Gotama: And what will you give those who survive these initial shocks?

Jesus: Then they learn that it pleases my Father to let the sun shine and rain fall on good

48

and wicked alike, that all their efforts at becoming superior men have been wrong-headed, and especially wrong-hearted, since they have not grasped what it is to be perfect as my heavenly Father is perfect.

Gotama: Splendid! At this point of the wedding-feast they must be staggering from such a heavy wine. What is the next course?

Jesus: Once they have understood that all their efforts heretofore have been in vain, they are ready to be introduced to right effort.

Gotama: And what is that?

Jesus: Right effort is no effort. The seed sprouts and grows by itself, whether they sleep or wake, in ways they know not.

Gotama: Truly you are the son of my heart! Who has understood me half so well as you? For this you receive the robe and the bowl.

Jesus: But there is still more to unlearn. So far only the outermost shell has cracked. There is still an inner lining to peel away before the fruit is made free.

Gotama: You mean the main course has not yet been served? Go on.

Jesus: It hurts to have the shell cracked - but if only they weren't so serious about them-selves, if only they could learn the play-fulness of God! It is, after all, a wedding-feast of which we speak.

Gotama: For some reason I am reminded of an inci-dent concerning one of my better pupils, Nan-in. Once a young physician visited him wishing to learn how to overcome the fear of death. Nan-in told him not to waste his time with Buddhism but to go home and take care of his patients. The young physician kept returning, however, always with the same request, and Nan-in would always tell him to stop wasting his time and to get on with the care of his patients. After much stubborn persistence, the young physician finally grasped the point. Because of his seriousness he was prevented from becoming serious. When at last he learned not to take himself so seriously, whether he lived or died, he was able to begin taking his patients seriously, whether they lived or died.

Jesus: But someone is sure to ask how he can take seriously in another what he fails to take seriously in himself.

Gotama: Perhaps he no longer takes either himself or the other seriously, but only "it". Freed from care about himself, a care which absorbed all his energy, he is now free to care at large. It is no longer beings he cares for but Being. When he dies another will take his place. If what he cares for is Being, what does the tiny transition point between his being and that of another matter, so long as Being persists. He can observe his passing like the fall of a leaf to the ground, where in death it may warm and nourish the earth beneath the winter snow.

Jesus: But doesn't this also empty his profession of all seriousness and urgency? What does it matter if his patients sicken and die so long as Being persists?

Gotama: It does *not* matter. In fact, in that sense he can no longer take seriously either his person or his work. So why does he continue to work, with more energy than ever? Let me put it this way: now he begins to work like the poet or the painter. He no longer seeks to change the world but to celebrate it. It is his way of praising Being. He loves to see Being thrive in beings. He loves to see beings enjoy the radiant presence of Being. By contrast, have you ever thought how doomed to unhappiness and frustration are those physicians who *do* take their work seriously, who seriously seek to conquer disease and death? Where do they find the motivation to carry on?

Jesus: You are right in saying that the only reality is Being. It alone is serious and all the rest is jest. Yes, the young physician will be truly happy if what he loves is Being. His happiness no one can take away. But consider this: suppose it happened that Being itself should fall in love with beings. Suppose Being took beings seriously. What would happen then?

Gotama: You speak of Being as though it were a person, an individuality.

Jesus: The only one, strictly speaking. Who alone is not trapped in selfishness and cut off from reality by concern over this own individuality, since that individuality is Being itself. Being is my Father's secret name.

Gotama: Does it make sense that Being should fall in love with beings, that eternity should cherish time?

51

Jesus: Of course not. But then I've never believed that the world had to make human sense. Perhaps it makes a higher sense that appears to our poor brains as nonsense.

Gotama: Tell me more of your nonsense world.

Jesus: Suppose a young man about the same age as your young physician, one who is terribly afraid of death, leaves his home to seek adventure. It may seem strange that someone afraid of death would turn adventurous, but we know that the fear of death takes many forms, and here the fear of death takes the form of fear of missing something in life. Who knows what lies beyond the farthest hills he can see from home? So he sets out to discover the other side of those hills. He meets new people, hears strange languages, feasts his eyes on all the sights, he experiments with all sorts of novelties. Eventually he runs out of money and he has to seek a job. Having to work puts a damper on his enjoyment and isolates him from his newfound friends. While they are partying he has to work. He gets left out and takes to drinking and drugging himself rather heavily to offset his disappointment. As a result he soon loses the job he has grown to hate. Now there is nothing left to do but hustle and try to support his habits. His loneliness deepens and with it his desperation. He is caught at petty thieving and spends some sobering months in jail. Where to go from there? What kind of job can he hope to get with his record? He thinks back on the old days at home. It seems like a dream now, a lost paradise, while the real world narrows into a dead-end in some garbage heap.

52

Gotama: But that paradise would have remained his
if only he had not grasped for it so desperately.

Jesus: It can be his again if only he opens his arms
to it. By seeking he cannot find, but why
should he search for what has already and
has always been given?

Gotama: Now we understand one another again.
Paradise is here now in every present
moment.

Jesus: Paradise is a heart greater than our heart, a
heart ever turned toward us even when we
turn away from ourselves in sheer disgust.
Paradise is there when the young man
turns back homeward, hoping only to find
some slavework, enough to eke out a living,
and finds instead his father running to greet
him with open arms.

Paradise is, instead of judgement, loving
reconciliation.

Gotama: Paradise is there when, upon embracing the
long-absent one, he loses himself in the
embrace.

Jesus: Paradise is a golden ring upon his finger,
instead of humiliation and rejection, and
wine, song, and feasting.

Gotama: But one thing troubles me: you continue to
speak of Being as a person, an individuality.
I have always hesitated to use those terms,
the idea of self being the illusion which
keeps us trapped in illusion, cutting us off
from Being. It is why I so responded to your
word: "How happy are those who know that
they are poor, for theirs is the kingdom of

Heaven." How happy are those who have seen through the illusion of the self, the personality, the separate individuality, for they have discovered Being! But if they must get beyond self to discover Being, how can you think of Being as characterized by selfhood?

Jesus: Your approach is very philosophical. It is not my want to use that language, but since you wish it I shall try; forgive me if from time to time I lapse into homely comparisons. Perhaps what is needed is not so much to drop the notion of personality and individuality as to revise it . . . though your long silence on the subject of God and the soul is better than the glib alternative. Have you noticed how the personality turned in on itself, the individuality careful to preserve itself, seems to shrivel, harden and die?

Gotama: Of course I have noticed it. Have I not analyzed the sickness in detail in order to find a remedy?

Jesus: But then it follows, does it not, that to go forth from the prison of the self towards the other is not to lose one's person but rather to have it grow immeasurably rich.

Gotama: Of course the movement we call love allows one to grow immeasurably rich, but since love lies in going forth, so long as growth continues there can be no return to one's own individual isolation and self-hood. Wouldn't a return mean a withdrawal from love?

Jesus: The return is the original discovery of love.
It is only in the return that we realize what
has taken place in the going forth. In going
forth we come to know the beloved and
when we return we come to know the love,
and ourselves transfigured by that love.
How would you have come to realize your
enlightenment had you not made the
return, and how would you have come to
teach if you had not only reached enlightenment but also realized that you had
reached it? You have emphasized going
forth, and with reason, for this first
movement is so difficult to make. What is
more difficult than to let go, let fall, let be,
look, listen, touch? And the second movement seems to be simplicity itself. We sum-
mon up all our courage, all our daring for
going forth, while the return happens of
itself almost without our noticing. Yet
there is an original return which may not be
so easy, which is perhaps more difficult and
decisive than the first movement. It is even
prior to the first movement.

Gotama: A first before the first?

Jesus: A movement so secret that we don't always
recognize it as a movement, a receiving of
the seed which precedes our coming to be.
Where do we find the courage for that
initial going forth, what secret substance
relaxes the death-grip on self in the first
surrender, what inspires the trust that lets
It be?

Gotama: I sense that we have now reached the
innermost fastness of your kingdom.

55

Jesus: It is very simple and very nonsensical, as you have noted already. It is what the young man discovers on his original return, the return homeward. It is the welcome where he had expected rejection, it is freedom where he had expacted a dead-end, it is bliss where he had expected only chargrin. It is the discovery that he is loved first and unconditionally which will enable the young man to make the first movement. It is because Being has already gone forth to beings that beings are enabled to experience Being in the going forth to one another.

Gotama: So, the final secret is that Being has fallen in love with beings.

Jesus: What is first in the universe is the last thing we discover.

Gotama: And this nonsense is the ground of all sense, the only seriousness.

Jesus: On that one pivot of earnestness the whole world can afford to turn in jest.

Gotama: It reminds me of the story of Ryokan, so poor that when the thief broke into his hut there was nothing there to steal. Ryokan, not wishing him to be disappointed, offered the thief his clothes. The thief took them and slunk away, perplexed and ashamed. Ryokan, sitting naked, mused to himself, "poor fellow, too bad I couldn't give him this beautiful moon as well."

Jesus: Ah, you have grasped it, of course you have. A man who has inherited a kingdom can afford to sit naked in the moonlight, can he not?

THE FOURTH DIALOGUE

IV

*It is night in Jerusalem, where Jesus has
come with friends to celebrate the Feast of
Tabernacles. Jesus finds himself confronted
daily by enemies, or by enthusiasts who
support him for all the wrong reasons. He
is weary of controversy, stupidity, shallow-
ness, meanness. He walks the dark streets
of Jerusalem alone. After a time he senses
the presence of another, walking beside him.*

Gotama: I thought you might want a chance to un-
burden your heart this evening.

Jesus: I might have known you would come,
Gotama. You always seem to sense my
need, often before I know it myself.

Gotama: This is one of the beauties of friendship.
Odd how I never thought of myself as any
man's friend, nor allowed another man to
call himself my friend, yet the joys of
friendship have never been lacking for me.

Jesus: Friendship without friends? Tonight you
will have to tell me this in plainer language.

Gotama: Of course. Isn't there something rather
pretentious in the thought of befriending
another man - as though we have something
to give another which he does not already
possess, as though he were in any way
lacking what he needs?

Jesus: You seem to make light of friendship, which
surprises me. I see you so full of compassion
for the suffering of others. Compassion is
the meaning of your life and way.

Gotama: It is true that I feel with the suffering of others, just as my heart goes out to you now in your suffering. Freed myself from the bondage of sorrow, why shouldn't I be of whatever assistance I can be to others who are still caught in that tangle? But my assistance does not spare a man the necessity of disentangling himself. He must still by himself remove the threads of illusion and delusion one by one. I am only a signpost on the way each man must walk for himself and by himself.

Jesus: Gotama, you are a humble man. Though there is sober truth in what you say, I wonder if you do not underestimate yourself vastly.

Gotama: This is still another reason why I cannot claim to be any man's friend. Don't you see that we place altogether too much importance and value on this small person of ours, which is nothing but the complex web of all our illusions, spun from ignorance of the truth? It is when we no longer pretend to give or seek to receive that friendship can be enjoyed.

Jesus: You are saying then that the self, the person does not matter, that it is itself an illusion?

Gotama: The sense of the self is the absolute source of illusion, the heart of ignorance and bondage. When we are freed of that, we are truly free.

Jesus: And I was beginning to think that little divided us. You see, I know that the self is not only valuable but of infinite, irreplace-

60

able value. Far from being the source of illusion, I see it as the source of truth.

Gotama: Infinite value? The source of truth? Indeed our differences are great if you mean what you say. I hope we can understand one another. I was deeply heartened when I heard you say that men must leave self behind to follow along the way, but I was disturbed when you added that to follow the way was to follow *you*. Your way of putting it confuses the issue - which is a question of leaving all self behind, myself, yourself, all selves, the whole notion of self. You would do better to distinguish clearly between your person and your teaching. Don't you see that that confusion is the source of all the controversy you find yourself in right now?

Jesus: I have often wondered at how your life unfolded in peace while mine arouses such disturbance and hatred.

Gotama: Exactly. It is because - if you will pardon my saying it - you attach such importance to your person, where what really matters is your message.

Jesus: Will it shock you if I say that my message is myself? I have nothing else to offer.

Gotama: It does shock me. It disturbs me profoundly to hear you speak so. I had thought you a man of great enlightenment, one far beyond such petty concerns.

Jesus: And so you too are scandalized at me, Gotama? But I know you to be a man of profound enlightenment, a man entirely

61

detached from self-interest. Relying on that detachment I ask you to hear me out. Others turn away offended where my claims bump up against their own pretensions. But since you have truly cleared away all self-conceit, perhaps you will listen with your empty and purified heart.

Gotama: I am ready to hear you.

Jesus: Let me say what I have to say in the form of a question. Which requires greater self-renunciation, to understand you or to believe in me?

Gotama: Now it is my turn to ask you to speak in plain language.

Jesus: A prophet said of me that my business among men was to lay bare the secret thoughts of many hearts. It is in their relationship to me that men's deepest thoughts are revealed.

Gotama: Your meaning is still hidden from me. But I shall return to the original question: which is more difficult? I only know that most men find it not at all easy to abandon the thought of self and its cravings, but once the fateful step is made their ease is unending.

Jesus: You say that you were heartened when I spoke of leaving self behind, but once again disheartened when I asked men to follow me. I say now that following me is the most radical form of self-renunciation.

Gotama: Forgive me if I still cannot grasp your language. When I speak of leaving self behind, I mean not only this particular self, but all notion of self, whether particular or universal, human or devine. You seem to be asking men to renounce themselves in order to cleave to another self, your own, which becomes a new world, an all-encompassing self for them - your desires in the place of their desires, your thoughts in place of their thoughts.

Jesus: When you put it that way I can see why they say that I am possessed and raving. It sounds like the ambition of a self-obsessed madman.

Gotama: I am sorry to say it, but it does.

Jesus: It is a frightful thing to see oneself as God.

Gotama: Wouldn't a humble posture be more reasonable and more sane?

Jesus: Strange as it may sound, to take my place as God is the humblest stance of all.

Gotama: Your words are now even more baffling.

Jesus: When a singular man of a given height and weight, of limited culture, and a mere thirty years of life experience, steps forth and announces that he is God, he is hurling in the face of other men the most terrible challenge - terrible for them and terrible for himself. Terrible for himself because by declaring his own Godhead he foregoes the handicaps which might be granted other men, or so it seems. A merciless light is trained upon him to show up his every flaw. Nothing is forbidden in the struggle against him for, after all, he can counter with the power of God. No pity is shown him, for God should not stand in need of human

63

pity. But it is terrible for those who struggle against him as well. Terrible for them because in whatever way they react to "the mere man" on whom they train their spotlight, they show for all to see what they really think about themselves, about their own mere manhood.

Gotama: But what they are reacting against is one particular individual raising himself to such heights. Why should you be God and not some other man?

Jesus: Why should I indeed? It is not I who am refusing to recognize the God in them, but they who refuse to acknowledge the God in me. I have reminded them that Scripture declares: "I said: you are gods."

Gotama: Then why not direct their gaze to the God in each one of them instead of to yourself. It would seem far less confusing and far easier to take.

Jesus: That it would be so much easier to take is an indication that, as a matter of fact, it would only be more confusing. Ask yourself why it would be easier and then you will see my point.

Gotama: I can see that it is far more difficult to recognize God in another than in oneself. Not being in the grip of another's illusion of self, one is quicker to perceive another's shortcomings and biases than one's own.

Jesus: Another man's pretensions are difficult to stomach; one's own are sweet and alluring.

Gotama: I can see that yours can be a way of bringing men up hard against the prison of self.

64

But is there not a danger involved as well?

Jesus: What is that?

Gotama: Some men are all too ready to identify one set of finite traits with the Godhead, particularly when they exercise a certain attractive power as I see in you. But I can see crowds of deluded fanatics following a deluded maniac, who has fooled himself as well as them.

Jesus: The misunderstanding of enthusiasts is every bit as great as that of those who are put off by the claims. It may be harder to correct. The problem occurs when God is recognized in one man but not in all, or is identified with one trait or set of traits. It is only when God is recognized in the most unlikely of traits and the most unlikely of men - and, of course, what that unlikeliness consists in differs from man to man - that His true features are discerned. One way or another, it is always a surprise, always a source of consternation, always it demands a leavetaking from one's old thoughts and values.

Gotama: And you think this leavetaking is more far-reaching than what I propose? You do not think it disturbing to men to be told that they are trapped in their own ignorance, and that what they value most has no value at all?

Jesus: On the contrary, Gotama. I know well that men find it very hard to acknowledge their stupidity, their limitations in whatever form. I am saying that it is harder still to love those limitations, to bless them, to cherish them.

Gotama: You have lost me again. Why would any man in his right mind bless and cherish the trap in which he is caught?

Jesus: At first he will probably thrash against it with rage and hatred in his heart - much as you see them striking out against me. Then he will disbelieve it, simply refuse it as absurd, ignore it and hope it will go away. But an honest man cannot keep up that pretense forever. He keeps knocking up against the walls of his prison in his attempts to escape. Life offers any number of little reminders. Then, faced with what he can no longer avoid, he despairs. He stares at the encroaching walls with the vacant stare of the heartbroken. And it may be, just may be, that as he fingers the harsh contours of those barriers, studying their ugly detail, he may see something new, something he had not noticed before. He may discover the piteous Face of God.

Gotama: How is it that the ugly turns out to be the beautiful?

Jesus: He finds the link that binds him to all other men, and the barriers dissolve. Not that he ceased to be a man afflicted with limitations, but he is no longer trapped in them. If he is able to acknowledge and accept his short-comings, the shortcomings of other men will no longer be an obstacle for him. He will have found the ability to love where before he could not help but despise.

Gotama: You have found a way to release men from the prison of self. Yours is the way of the great affirmation and mine the way of the great negation. They sound like opposite ways, but both achieve complete release, both succeed in bringing everything into unity. I wonder if there is not some point where language, which divides into 'this' and 'that', which cannot affirm and at the same time negate, cannot negate and at the same time affirm, fails. The only thing that matters, after all, is release from the hell of egotism.

Jesus:　The only thing that matters is the discovery of love.

Gotama:　You see, I speak the language of the mind and you speak the language of the heart. The question is whether a man's understanding can be transformed without a corresponding change of heart, and whether his heart can be healed without transfiguring vision?

Jesus:　You think that way entails mine and mine yours?

Gotama:　You spoke of rage and thrashing, avoidance and despair. It is what I had in mind when I declared that existence is pain, pain reinforced and fed by the desire to be what we are not, desire reinforced and fed by not realizing that we are doing just that — reinforcing and feeding our pain by refusing it. It is that ignorance I propose to cure. I show a way to end the desire to be other than what we are. The extinguishing of that desire is simply the other side of that profound acceptance which you refer to as God.

Jesus: When you put it that way, Gotama, it does seem so. Still, if it is so, I do not understand why my hearers wish to destroy me while no such hatred was trained on you.

Gotama: Could it be because I speak the language of those who have not yet stepped over the threshold, reminding them of their ignorance which they can understand, while you speak from within the house, reminding them of their sin which they cannot understand?

Jesus: That threshold is the discovery that we are both god and sinner. Everything is affirmed and everything is denied simultaneously.

Gotama: All men can understand human language, if they will, but only those who have crossed over can understand divine.

Jesus: Looking back from within a warm and well-lighted house a man realizes clearly that the rage and thrashing, the darkness and despair were sin, the struggle against love.

Gotama: But standing outside looking in, his torment is made unbearable by all talk of God and sin.

Jesus: Have I then made a great mistake, Gotama, in describing the beauty of that house to those still lost in the night?

Gotama: I think that one who has left the comforts of his house to go out to those in darkness has earned the right to speak.

Jesus: Even if they cannot hear?

Gotama: You have come to reveal the secret thoughts of hearts, regardless of what those secret thoughts may be. How can there be a revelation of the very beautiful without a corresponding revelation of the very ugly?

Jesus: If only it were an abstract teaching, and the lives of men were not at stake!

Gotama: No, cruel as it may seem, you do men a great favor in unveiling the blackness of their hearts. It is the shock of that self-discovery which explodes the prison walls. With the collapse of the idea of self comes the release into compassion. Those who fail to make the discovery, who refuse it, not only in the first moments of reeling and staggering from the blow, but who turn deaf ears and blind eyes, they remain in their deafness and blindness, and that is their woe. For them the revelation has never occurred.

Jesus: Yes, Gotama, I see what you mean. It comes for each man when the time is right.

Gotama: Infallibly.

Jesus: At that precise moment when he reaches the fullness of time.

Gotama: And passes over into eternity.

Jesus: When he accepts his whole past, his whole present, his whole future.

Gotama: When he accepts the world's past, the world's present, the world's future.

Jesus: Until that moment arrives for him time
          continues to escape him - the past has
          vanished, the future is not yet, the present
          is abstract. Locked out of eternity, he is
          locked out of time as well.

THE FIFTH DIALOGUE

V

It is the Monday before Passover, Jesus is alone for the first time in days. He has just left a dinner at which Mary, in an impulsive and spontaneous gesture, anointed his head and feet. The gesture was surprising and shocked several of the guests. Jesus knows that it is a sign: Mary has unknowingly anointed him for burial. He understands that his death is not far now.

Gotama: I hope I am not disturbing your thoughts.

Jesus: On the contrary, today of all days, I find it good to talk with you. I have had an uncanny experience - one which I cannot share with many, with those who would be too frightened by it.

Gotama: You have seen your death.

Jesus: I have received a signal. I have had them before, but more frequently of late.

Gotama: Are you afraid?

Jesus: Not yet - but fear may come. For the moment I am filled with awe and a strange exaltation.

Gotama: What did you see or hear? Can you describe it?

Jesus: A woman, a friend of mine, for no apparent reason broke a jar of very expensive ointment and anointed my body with it. The companions were dumbfounded. I too was taken by surprise, but I knew at once that it was a message from my Father.

Gotama: A message from your Father? So many men

73

have wondered what death looks like and what message it brings. It is said that our death lurks behind us at all times, that if we glance back very quickly we can sometimes catch sight of it. Those who have seen it call it the being without a face. It stands behind us with an upraised hatchet. But for most men the horror lies not in the threat of the hatchet, but in the facelessness.

Jesus: No man in this life has ever seen the Father's face. He could be the faceless being you describe. Yet I have never thought of His presence in the shuddering manner of which you speak.

Gotama: Nature abhors a vacuum; we rush to fill it with our own projections. Some men paint that face with their fears, some with wishes. Many alternate in their fantasy between nightmare and pleasant dream. If it has never caused you to shudder, I take it that you paint only in bright colors. Or maybe you have no fears?

Jesus: Our tradition recognizes that God is at once terrible and beautiful. He destroys and He brings to life. What is important, however, is not so much the face one sees but the way of relating to it.

Gotama: I could not agree with you more! In fact, I am surprised and delighted to find us in agreement on this point. Most men make the great mistake of attaching all the importance to the face presented; they argue with one another over which is the true face, never realizing that the many faces of God are of their own making.

74

Jesus: If a man sees only one face, he reduces God to human size. In fact, he makes God less than human, for men have rich natures and can exhibit many faces. He turns God into a wooden statue, a cardboard figure, a caricature.

Gotama: Little does he realize that by caricaturing God, requiring of Him an intolerable and boring consistency, he is improverishing himself in the same manner and to the same degree. His own life becomes rigid and sterile.

Jesus: But if he sees the many faces of God, or recognizes God in the many and even conflicting visions, he remains in touch with all facets of himself, and with the tension which generates life in all of its variety.

Gotama: And so you are able to recognize your God in the upraised hatchet as well as in the hand raised in blessing. Tell me, by what mark do you know that this is really God?

Jesus: Every mark in His mark: He is always present. It is not a matter of finding Him in some things or events and not in others.

Gotama: But you spoke of a special signal.

Jesus: Throughout life man is given reminders of death, but when the configuration occurs he knows that it is near.

Gotama: What sort of configuration?

Jesus: There is a configuration at the beginning and a configuration at the end. Each points to a fullness: good and evil come together, and so do inner and outer events. Yet they are

75

not identical: rather, they mirror one another. For example, when I was born the
astrologers saw a great star; as a result,
violence erupted and many innocent children were killed. Now violence and hatred
take the lead and plot my death; as a result
there will be an eruption of great light.

Gotama: Do you think something similar occurs at
each person's beginning and end?

Jesus: It occurs, but is seldom perceived. Each
life and death hold a promise of fullness.
All too often it goes unnoticed because of
inattentiveness.

Gotama: I have taught that a man cannot become
fully enlightened without recollecting his
past lives. I wonder now if there is not a
likeness between our methods. If we think
of a man's life as a crossroads, whether we
pay attention to all the forces coming to
meet at the center point or trace the many
converging roads back to their points of
origin, the result is the same . . . an awareness of a fullness, a coming together of
everything.

Jesus: What makes the difference between people
is not so much the contents of life - what
things have happened - but rather a difference
in awareness, the way people relate to the
contents of life.

Gotama: I believe that becoming aware of past
lives is only a preliminary step. A man sees
what has been done and what has been left
undone. The two together make a whole, a
fullness as you say, like the bright and dark
sides of the moon. Real enlightenment

76

does not come, however, with the vision of fullness. It comes in learning how to stop the moon, how to put an end to her perpetual waxing and waning, how to become free.

Jesus: Tell me how you relate to the faces of God.

Gotama: A man must turn and look into the faces of God as they present themselves, one by one. He must stare hard until he learns the secret of each one. It does not matter whether he begins with the beautiful faces or the terrible faces. Suppose be begins with the terrible. He must not be afraid, he must not recoil or run away. He must study the horror in all its gruesome detail. But then he must realize - and here is what makes the man of enlightenment - it is I who have shaped this face. Its cruelty and ugliness are manufactured from the ingredients of my own soul. I am looking at my own face. I am looking in a spotless mirror.

Jesus: Terrible thought!

Gotama: I thought few men can sustain.

Jesus: Does he now despair?

Gotama: As I have said, he must not recoil, he must not run away. He must push thought to its furthest limit. He must think to himself: danger does not lie without, danger lies within. Destruction does not come from without, destruction comes from within. If I have shaped these awful faces, it is up to me to destroy them.

Jesus: But how can he do so?

Gotama: He says to himself: these are my fears, these

my suspicions, these my doubts, these my
resentments. I recognize them now. I am
taking them back home, back to my soul
from which they sprang. I am like a child
in a dark room, seeing goblins and monsters
in every flitting shadow.

Jesus: And like the child, he is reassured when he
realizes that the evil beings are but the
product of his own morbid fancy.

Gotama: Exactly, but now, somewhat reassured, he
must continue to gaze into the mirror while
his soul tries to reassure him completely by
spinning out beautiful dreams in place of the
nightmares. As he studies the beautiful
faces of God, he must not allow himself to
be drawn towards them, he must not
relinquish himself to the offering of the
embrace. He must hold himself in check. He
must study the beauty in all its seductive
detail. But then he must realize - and here
is what makes the man of enlightenment -
it is I who have shaped this face. Its loveli-
ness and its desirability are manufactured
from the ingredients of my own soul. I am
looking at my own face. I am looking in a
spotless mirror.

Jesus: Another terrible thought!

Gotama: And again, a thought few men can sustain.
Still a man must not let himself be drawn,
he must not relinquish himself. He must
push thought to its furtherest limit. He
must think to himself: salvation does not
lie without, salvation lies within. Bliss does
not come from without, bliss comes from
within. If I have shaped these lovely faces,

it is up to me to destroy them.

Jesus: But why should he do so?

Gotama: He says to himself: These are my wishes, these my hopes, these my compensations. I recognize them now. I am taking them back home, back to the soul from which they sprang. I am like a child in a sandbox, building castles and peopling them with imaginary princes and princesses.

Jesus: And like the child, tired of playing, he stamps on his sandcastle and takes a child's delight in the stamping?

Gotama: Yes, for now he has the lightheartedness of a child, being freed from hopes and fears.

Jesus: And is that how you would have the enlightened man face death, free from hope and fear?

Gotama: Now he is able to see death in truth. He knows that whatever he sees in death, whatever message it brings him, is a product of his own fancy. Death is silent; it has no face. A man looking into that mirror casts no reflection. It is the face you had before your mother conceived you. Can you look at it?

Jesus: What does a man gain by staring into emptiness, Gotama?

Gotama: Freedom. It is no small prize. Let me tell you a story to explain the benefits. Once upon a time there was a poor boy, the son of a woodcutter, who had to interrupt his studies because he had no money. He returned home to help his father, and one day

79

while he was in the woods he heard a voice calling for help. He followed the sound and came to a great oak tree in the middle of the forest. The voice cried, "help! Let me out!" It seemed to be coming from the roots of the oak tree. He dug down and found a beautiful old bottle, perfectly round, of a transparent golden glass. The voice was trapped within. The boy uncorked the bottle and a spirit rushed out, expanded mightily, and announced that he must strangle the one who released him. The boy, thinking quickly, said: "First, I have the right to know whether you are the same spirit who was in the bottle." To prove that he was the very same, the spirit slipped back into the bottle, and the boy quickly corked it. When the spirit clamored for his release, the boy was shrewd enough to make him promise a good reward. The spirit gave him a small piece of cloth, one side of which turned whatever it touched to silver and gold. With the help of the marvelous cloth the boy became a rich and powerful physician.

Jesus: So, by means of his wit the boy transmuted the forces of death into a source of power and wealth.

Gotama: The evil spirit is just one of the many faces of God which emerge from the soul. Any one of them, whether terrible or beautiful has the power when unleashed to strip a man of his life . . . But if the man knows how to outwit the spirit and coax it back into the bottle, then he can gain control over that power and have it serve him. It is done

80

by pushing understanding to its limit; That is why it is called "enlightenment." The paradox is that the supreme achievement of understanding is to will its own downfall - the attempt to think what cannot be thought. Having seen and seen through the many faces of God, it stands before the faceless being. You see, in reality there is only one spirit to coax back into the bottle - the understanding itself. It is by relinquishing himself in his highest capacity that a man becomes truly free. No longer captive to his own illusions and delusions, he has the supreme freedom of movement which no amount of wealth can buy. Healed from ignorance and craving, he is a source of healing for all mankind. What can death take from the man who has already thrown away all his goods? Who is there to die?

Jesus: You have disarmed death, Gotama, by offering in advance all that death would take away. At the same time, you have honored life by raising understanding to its highest power. In one and the same moment a man reaches his highest achievement and relinquishes all achievement.

Gotama: And from that moment on he is free.

Jesus: Our ways are similar, but different.

Gotama: In what sense?

Jesus: I, too, would have a man learn all the faces of God, the terrible and the beautiful. I too would have him realize that those many faces mirror his own soul. Yet I would not have him simply dispel those faces as illusions; I would also ask him to recognize each and all of them as true God and true man. You speak of neither recoiling nor embracing, but I would have him both recoil from and embrace each and every one - embrace the beautiful but also embrace the terrible, recoil from the terrible but also recoil from the beautiful. Negate and affirm it all. Again there is a relinquishing of the understanding since the understanding cannot comprehend incompatibles, but there is a gift of the heart as well. That to which the heart is given in death is what I call my Father.

Gotama: Then for you death - what I have called the faceless being - is not the Father himself?

Jesus: Death is the giving or, in instances of failure, it is a taking away. The Father is that to which the heart is given. All of a man's life has to do with the forming of his heart. The gift of his heart is what is called spirit. The only failure in life is to die heartlessly.

Gotama: Of this I am sure, your death will not be a heartless affair. I have always thought of death as the supreme moment of truth. You must think of it as the supreme moment of love. But is there finally a difference between truth and love?

Jesus: I think I can best explain it by a story - in fact, a slightly different version of the story you told. It goes like this. Once there was a poor but talented boy, the son of a humble woodcutter, who lived at the edge of a mighty forest. Because of bad times he had to re-nounce his studies and return home to help his father gain a living. One day walking alone in the forest he heard a voice crying: "Help! Let me out!" He followed the voice and

82

found that it was coming from the roots of
a giant oak tree. He dug down between the
roots and discovered a beautiful old bottle,
perfectly round, and made of transparent
golden glass. Yes, the voice was certainly
coming from within the bottle. His heart
was touched by the plaintiveness of its pleas.
It was this, and not curiosity which finally
persuaded him to open the bottle, though
since it had no cork, he was forced to
shatter the ancient and beautiful thing.
Break it he did upon a stone. It shattered
musically like fine crystal and at once a
mighty spirit rose up, expanded, and
announced with a loud harsh voice that it
must now strangle its rescuer. The boy's
hands were bleeding where they had been
cut in several places by the fine slivers of
glass. The boy considered for a moment,
then said: "But I am not certain that you
are the same spirit I released. Your voice is
so different now. The bottle is gone, but if
you can constrict yourself into my cupped
hands, I will believe that you are the same
spirit." To prove that he was the very same,
the spirit compressed himself into the boy's
bleeding hands. But when it came into
contact with the blood a marvelous change
came over the terrible spirit. When it cried
out, "You see, I am the very same!," its
voice had lost all harshness. The boy responded,
"Ah, I recognize you now, you are in truth
the spirit I released. My heart was touched
with pity by your voice. Now if your release
can be had only through my death, you have
my permission." But the spirit found itself
unable to carry through its terrible design. It
was appalled to have ever cherished such a

thought. Instead it gave to the boy its greatest treasure - a wondrous cloth, one side of which rubs away every wound and the other side of which turns whatever it touches to silver and gold.

Gotama: You say that I have disarmed death, but I say that you have transformed it. You must go now to your high destiny.

THE SIXTH DIALOGUE

VI

Gethsemane. Jesus' companions are asleep. Simon, James, and John, his closest friends, do not understand the horror he faces. He staked everything on the Father's love, but now terror rolls over him like a storm. Gotama comes towards him from the shadows.

Jesus: Gotama, I am ashamed for you to see me. I am deathly afraid, ready to run. It seems to me that I have already betrayed all that I hold most dear.

Gotama moves out of the shadows towards Jesus. Jesus sees that there is a large white flower floating in the cup Gotama bears.

Gotama: It is the lotus which grows in murky waters while keeping its petals unsoiled. Your fears and doubts are like the water. They have no power to stain the essence of mind unless you yourself allow it.

Gotama offers the cup to Jesus. Jesus takes it with both hands and gazes deeply into its contents. Slowly he lifts the lotus from the cup and returns it to Gotama, who receives it with reverence. Jesus lifts the cup to his lips and drains it at one draught. The figure of Gotama begins to shift. Is it an effect of the dark potion? The figure changes. Now Mary of Bethany stands before him. How has she come to be here?

Mary: I could not let you go like this. You are destroying yourself senselessly.

Jesus: Mary, I thought you were reconciled to my going.

Mary: How can I be reconciled to folly? Why
          must you be so much in love with this
          inflated image of yourself? You don't
          love me or anyone else, only yourself, only
          a mirage of yourself.

Jesus: That tone is so unlike you, Mary. You
          baffle me. I hardly know how to respond to
          you now, you seem so far away. Don't
          you remember the beautiful moment when
          you anointed me as though for burial? I
          took it to mean that you understood.

Mary: What is there to understand? You have
          brought all this on yourself with your
          foolish ideas and ambitions. And now you
          plan to have yourself martyred.

Jesus: You used to think my words and actions
          were real enough. Have you forgotten all
          that we have shared?

Mary: You are the one who has forgotten every-
          thing! If you loved me you would think
          of my feelings. Am I not to be considered
          in your decision to live or to die?

Jesus: You look the same, Mary, yet I don't
          recognize you. You are not the Mary who
          made me long to return to Bethany
          whenever I could. No, you must be some
          dark projection of my own soul, an
          effect of the bitter drink.

          *Once again the figure shifts. When Jesus
          looks again it is no longer the young Mary
          but the Magdalen who stands before him.*

Jesus: Mary, how have you come here?

Mary: Did you avoid telling me on purpose? Thank
          God, I heard of the developments before it
          was too late. Why have you left me like this
          without a word?

Jesus: Mary, I was sure that you at least would
          understand.

Mary: You avoided telling me because you would
          have to confess that you misled me. You
          could not face it.

Jesus: Mary, how can you speak this way? The
          recovery of the child in you, trusting and
          full of faith's vision, has been one of the
          greatest gifts of my life. And now to hear
          you speaking so cynically!

Mary: Well might I be cynical. You told me of a
          God whose very name is love, a faithful
          God, full of tenderness and pity, whose
          care for us is limitless, a lover of life who
          takes no pleasure in destroying what His
          own hands have made. What has become
          of that God now?

Jesus: No, the question is what has become of
          the Magdalen through whom the essence
          of God shone in unspeakable beauty? You
          are not she, but a caricature. I will speak
          with you no longer. Even at her unhappiest
          moments my Magdalen was full of beauty,
          though at times the beauty was obscured -
          but you are nothing but a hollow shell.

          *The figure blurs and vanishes. When Jesus
          looks up again his mother stands before
          him.*

Mary: My son, would you leave me without a
          word? I heard the rumors and my heart

89

stopped with fear. And when I heard further
that you were aware of the plot against you,
I was crushed by the thought that you had
left me to find it out from talk in the streets.

Jesus: I never thought of you as one to listen to
street talk. I think of my mother as listening
steadily to another voice, one which speaks
secretly from within and from beyond.

Mary: Are you not ashamed to leave your old
mother without even a word or a gesture
to draw comfort from in the years left to
her, years in which she will become feebler,
more helpless, more alone, more abandoned?

Jesus: I don't understand what is happening. All
three of you have turned into selfish,
destructive weights upon my soul. But
you shock me most of all. I do not recognize my mother in your whining. She is not
one to be moved by the rise and fall of
fortune, least of all by her own. She is not
one to be anxious for the future. Above all,
she is not one to think only of herself in
my dark hours. Whoever you are, you are
not she.

*The figure shifts again. Jesus cries out in
his distress. He recovers himself and looks
up again to see towering over him the
rugged figure of Elijah.*

Jesus: Father Elijah, have you come now, the
long-awaited guest, to comfort me with a
share of your spirit and power?

Elijah: Would that my mission were so pleasant.
Instead I have been sent to warn you of
your failure.

Jesus:	What do you mean, my father?
Elijah:	Upon you fell the mantle of the prophets. You were destined to lead Israel in the power and strength of Yahweh. Upon you the accumulated gifts of a high destiny have gathered. But where is the fruit of your labors? Are the people better off for your having come? Is there any evidence of the beginning of the messianic age? Will the ages to come be animated by a transformed spirit? Will the world be impressed by your power?
Jesus:	But, my father, for you God was not manifest in the mighty wind, nor in the earthquake, nor in fire. He showed himself in the still, small voice of a gentle breeze before which you covered your face in awe. Am I not faithful to that same God of Israel if the One I show forth can only be detected in the secret moment, the unspoken word, the swift glance? Our God is not heavy, not obvious. Our God is a lover of the hidden and the paradox.
Elijah:	Let me show you the ages to come, the future of your movement. See if your heart can bear the vision. Tell me if you detect the presence and power of God - even a subtle, paradoxical presence.

Jesus is caught up in a trance in which he sees the ages of Christianity unfold before him, all the individuals and movements that swear allegiance to his name, all the actions done and not done in his name, all the terrible interpretations of his message.

91

Elijah: I am sorry to have to show you this bitter outcome. Have you heart left to speak?

Jesus: I saw moments of tenderness, gestures of mercy, quiet endurance, hearts full of prayer, songs in the morning and songs in the evening, flashes of vision, and silence heavy with hope.

Elijah: Moments! A few seconds, brief flashes during long centuries of greed, exploitation, tyranny of the spirit, and unbridled cruelty! How is it that your eyes are not burned out of their sockets by what you saw?

Jesus: I do not understand you, my father. Have you forgotten your own experience of God? How is it that your mind and heart are overwhelmed by the gross failure? Do you not feel the gentle breeze quietly moving through those centuries, even in the midst of earthquake and fire? How can you be Elijah and not discern the Spirit of God? It is my turn to be surprised at you that you did not receive the vision of those centuries on your knees. But I think you are an imposter and no true prophet.

The figure swirls. The apparition is transformed into the majestic figure of Moses. Before the grandeur and radiance of Moses' countenance Jesus forgets that the previous visitations have been false. His soul is seized and held by the mighty vision.

Jesus: Father Moses, do you come bringing manna and water from the rock to strengthen me on my night journey?

Moses: I come to accuse you of destroying the

people for whom I gave my life and strength. I struggled with God for their sakes, begging Him to wipe me out of His book rather than turn upon them. But you choose to live at their expense. You let the ancient olive perish while you, the branch, have care to be transplanted to some wild growth where you can live on alone, forgetting your origins.

Jesus: Father Moses, if that were true I should have escaped weeks ago and left this people to their own devices. If I die tomorrow, it is because I have refused to leave my roots. It is one thing to tear oneself away, it is another to be cast out and disowned.

Moses: I promised them that another would come to take my place, a leader whom they were to follow implicitly. How I regret those words, for you have played them false! Where is the land for which they were destined? Has it materialized? You have given the lie to all God's promises. If you have the heart for it, let me show you the future of Judiasm, the ages of exile and abandonment, the heavy load of hatred and shame, and all because of you.

Once again Jesus falls into a trance and before his inward eye passed the destruction of Jerusalem, the diaspora, the centuries of suffering, persecution and murder.

Moses: Look, if you can bear it. Can you assume responsibility for this holocaust? What answer can you give to the curse of the dying? Why are you not willing, like any good shepherd, to lay down your life for the sheep rather than have them come to this?

Jesus: No, my father, I will not assume responsibility but I will make an answer. It is not I who misled them. It is true I promised them a land of their own, But I have also made it quite clear that my kingdom is not of this world.

Moses: Spiritual kingdoms, so much cloudy comfort! What they are looking for, and what they have a right to through their sufferings, is something real, a fulfillment in this world to compensate for all their wordly loss.

Jesus: Can you be the Moses who spoke with God face to face? Are you the Moses who destroyed the golden calf in wrath and shame, when the people determined to fashion for themselves a tangible god? No, you are totally unlike him despite the outward radiance wheich dazzles the eye. The true Moses shone from within and knew God's secret name. I will be fooled by you no longer.

Once more the figure shifts. Jesus shuts his eyes in silent dread. When he opens them there stands before him the hoary figure of Abraham, transparent and sweet with age.

Jesus: Father Abraham, of all men you are he whom I have most longed to see, you who are privileged to be called God's friend!

Abraham: My son, would that the circumstances of our meeting were happier. Through distant centuries I have longed for your coming.

94

Dear have you been to me because of the
beautiful vision which animated your soul.
You, my longed for son! How is it that at
the very last your vision failed you? How is
it that you lost faith in God and cried out
to Him in despair?

Jesus: Father of all believers, you of all men must
          know that faith has its mountains and its
          valleys, its seasons of abundance and its
          seasons of famine, its day and its night. Your
          own faith was no simpleminded and
          stubborn thing. In your story there were
          moments of darkness and doubt. Why do
          you not sympathize with my distress instead
          of accusing me?

Abraham: But have you not give the lie to the God
          you preached by thinking yourself abandoned?
          My God was one who called me out of my
          familiar surroundings, out into abandonment,
          the unknown. Your God is one who comes to
          meet you in every circumstance, no matter
          how familiar. It was not unusual for me to
          feel disoriented, but for you is it not a scandal?

Jesus: The God who calls us out is also the one who
          comes to meet us; the one who comes to
          meet is also the one who calls out. So
          the strange is within the familiar and the
          familiar within the strange. It is not unusual
          that sometimes we recognize Him and
          sometimes not.

Abraham: One would expect the Anointed of God to
          recognize Him always.

Jesus: You are harsh, Father Abraham, harsh
          where God is tender. He took pity on your
          distress and comforted you with signs and

95

reassurances. How is it that the friend of
God is not full of that same overflowing
pity? Despite the sweetness of your outward
appearance I find no sweetness within. You
give no evidence of knowing Him, far less of
being His familiar.

*The figure makes one last change. Jesus
feels it at the depth of his being. He is seized
with trembling and hardly dares open his
eyes. When he does, the vision is terrifying.
Before him stands one altogether like himself, but transfused with golden light.*

Jesus: Who are you?

The figure: I am Ben-Adam, the Son of Man. I am
none other than your very self, Lion of
Judah. The projections have now withdrawn
and it is given you to behold yourself
victorious, Prince, mighty warrior. You
have trampled your foes in the winepress.
Your garments are stained with their blood.
Now enjoy the fruit of your labors, conqueror.

Jesus: The only blood on my garments is my
own. It is true that I have stood firm
against accusations which would have sapped
my soul of its very life. Now it seems that I
must also stand firm against flattery.

The figure: You do not understand. The time of
delusion is over. You have withstood the
test. Now is the moment of triumph.

Jesus: I have discovered what it is to be a
human being among human beings, what
it is to be limited, uncertain, receiving far
more than I am able to give. I have discovered what it is to stumble and be lifted
up, what it is to be mistaken and erring
yet guided by a heart

96

greater than my own, what it is to have
little yet always enough for others as well
as myself.

The figure: You are weary from your many ordeals,
suffering Lamb of God. You have drunk to
its dregs the bitterness of the human
condition. Now are you to be rewarded
in the measure of your sufferings. Now are
you vindicated. Your accusers have been
reduced to silence. Now do you crush them
beneath your feet.

Jesus: How you do rave on! Don't you tire of all
those superlatives? I don't know who you
are but I believe you are in fact more
dangerous than those whom you call my
accusers. They attempted to cast guilt
and terror into my soul, but you would lure
me with the promise of sweetness, casting
over me an even heavier sleep. You are
nothing but an abstraction, grandeur without
lowliness, strength without weakness,
beauty without homeliness. I will have
nothing to do with you. No, you are not
the end of my striving. You are not the
one who sustains me in secret. Even in
victory He is humble. Though raised high
over all the earth his gaze rests upon the
poor man on his dungheap in whom He
finds delight.

*The figure dissolves. In its place, from all
directions, there grows a clear, white light.
The light comes from within Jesus as well
as from without. He is affirmed and held by
it. It lifts him and spreads him apart, atom
by atom. His body seems to be expanding
in every direction, taking on the dimensions*

*the universe. From far away he hears the
beloved voice of Gotama: "You have seen
through all the illusions and delusions as
benefits the Anointed of the Most High.
Now, Maitreya, go in peace to your appointed
place." Suddenly Jesus finds in his left hand
the perfect lotus, in his right the emptied
cup, their outreach touching the extremities
of space.*

JUXTAPOSITIONS

Gotama's father had surrounded his son with every luxury and was careful to see that he was shielded from any sight of life's misery. One day as he rode with his charioteer Gotama saw an old man, bent with age. "Who is that?" Gotama asked, shocked at his first sight of the infirmities age can bring. "It is an old man, sire," the charioteer replied. Gotama asked, "To whom does this terrible thing happen?" 'To all – every man, woman, and child." Gotama returned to the palace disturbed.

A few days later he was again in his chariot. By the roadside lay a man who was hopelessly ill. Gotama asked the charioteer to stop. "Who is this man?" "A sick man, sire. There is no cure for him."

Later they passed a funeral procession. Gotama asked, "Who are these people? Why are they weeping, and who are they carrying?" "A dead man, sire. His family and friends weep for him because he is gone from them forever."

Gotama thought, "This, then, is life! Youth into age, health into disease, all ending in death." He spent many days alone, and then went out again. With his charioteer he passed a man walking alone. His head was shaven, and he wore a yellow robe. When Gotama asked about him, his charioteer said, "He is a monk, sire, one who has gone forth," "And what is this going forth?' " The charioteer answered, "To go forth means living the religious life completely, living the peaceful life completely, living in complete kindness toward all living creatures." Gotama then determined to go forth and live the life of a monk, despite the wishes of his family.

When they finally found him, his mother
said: "My son, why have you treated us like
this? Didn't you know that we would be
desperate searching for you?" Jesus looked
at her and said, "Why did you search? Didn't
you realize that I was bound to be here in my
father's house?"

His family came to get him, for people were
saying he was insane. When they arrived they
sent in a message, and word went through the
crowd: "Your mother and brothers are outside
asking for you." He looked at those around him
and said: "Here is my mother and here are my
brothers. Whoever does the will of God is mother,
brother, and sister to me."

Gotama sat in deep meditation, determined not to
rise until he had attained enlightenment. Mara the demon
sought to tempt him with visions of earthly power and
delight. When these failed Mara attempted to terrify
him. Finally the demon confronted Gotama and demanded
that he stop. "Who do you think you are?" Mara roared.
"By what right do you seek the Supreme Enlightenment?
Who is your witness?" Gotama reached down with his
right hand to touch the earth and the earth shouted
with a voice of thunder, "I am your witness."

Jesus went out into the desert for
forty days and forty nights, and there
Satan tried to tempt him.

Jesus went down to the Jordan, where
John was baptizing those who wished to
confess their sins and change their lives.
When Jesus approached John was startled
and would have stopped him, but Jesus

102

told him he intended to follow the ordinary
way. So John baptized him. But when Jesus
came out of the water the Holy Spirit appear-
ed over his head in the form of a dove, and
a voice was heard saying "Thou art my son,
my beloved; on thee my favor rests."

Existence is pain.
Pain raises from desire.
Pain ceases when desire is extinguished.
Desire is extinguished by following the middle way.

I have come that you may have life, and
have it more abundantly.

This sickness is not due to this man's sin, or
his parents' sin, but instead exists so that
God's beauty may be revealed in the
healing.

Shall I not drink the cup which the Father
himself has given me?

I am the Way.

How can you laugh or rejoice
when the whole world is burning?
When darkness covers you,
why do you not look for a light?

If you are on the roof, don't go down to
get your things from the house. If you are
in the field, don't turn back for your coat.

Rise up! Be attentive! Follow the right way.
The one who follows the way is happy now and
forever.

Happy is the servant who, when his master
returns, is found watching.

"These are my sons; this is what I own."
So the fool torments himself with his thoughts.
He does not even belong to himself.
How can sons or wealth be his?

Jesus told them this story: "There was a
wealthy man whose harvest was so great
one year that he hardly knew what to do
with it. Finally he decided to tear down
his existing barns and build newer, bigger
ones. 'At last,' he thought to himself, 'I
have made it! I can take life easy now, have
a good time, and enjoy the fruits of my
labor.' What a fool! Little does he suspect
that this very night God will require his
soul of him. So it is with everyone who
amasses wealth for himself and remains
a pauper in the sight of God."

Look at this body — a painted image, miserable,
suffering, no strength to hold itself together.

Do not fear what kills the body and then
can do no more. Fear what destroys the
soul and casts it into hell.

The world is dark. Only a few see the light.
Only a few escape to heaven, as few birds escape
the net.

Broad is the road that leads to perdition;
many take it. Narrow is the road that leads
to salvation; few take it.

Better than power to rule the world,
better than going to heaven,
is one step on the way to Nirvana.

>What does it profit a man to gain the whole
>world and suffer the loss of his soul?

If a man in battle conquers thousands
and another man conquers himself,
his victory is greater .
One man makes thousands of sacrifices for a hundred
years.
Another for one moment honors an enlightened man
and he has done the greater thing.

>Whoever welcomes a prophet because he
>is a prophet will receive a prophet's reward.
>Whoever welcomes a just man because he
>is just will receive a just man's reward.

A man can sacrifice a whole year to gain merit,
but this is not worth one moment's reverence for a
righteous man.

>Whoever welcomes one of these little ones
>in my name welcomes me.

A blade of grass handled wrongly can cut the hand.
So asceticism, undertaken wrongly, can lead to hell.

>Jesus told a story aimed at those who were
>confident of their own goodness and
>scornful of others. "Two men went to the
>temple to pray. One was a Pharisee, the
>other a tax-gatherer. The Pharisee went
>right to the front and prayed, 'I thank you,
>God, that I am not like other men, selfish,
>cheating, loose-living. I fast twice a week,

105

I pay my tithes.' The tax-gatherer stayed at
the back and barely raised his eyes. He prayed,
'Have mercy on me, God, sinner that I am.'
I tell you, the gax-gatherer went home a free
man, the other not. Whoever exalts himself
will be humbled, and whoever humbles himself will be exalted."

Nakedness, matted hair, fasting, covering
oneself with dust and ashes, lying on nails
—none of these things can purify a man
if the mind is not pure.

> It is not what goes into or out of the body
> that soils a man. It is what comes forth
> from his heart.

If anyone harms another who is innocent
his evil returns to him,
like dust tossed against the wind.

> If someone slaps you on the right cheek,
> offer him the left as well.
> If someone demands your shirt, offer him
> your coat as well.

A man with no wound on his hand may touch
poison without harm; and the man who is not
evil cannot be harmed by evil.

> Love your enemies; do good to those who
> hurt you.
> Be children for your heavenly Father,
> who makes the sun shine on good and bad
> alike, who gives the gentle rain to both
> honest and dishonest.

All beings fear punishment, all fear death.
Remember you are like them: do not kill,
or cause killing.

Love one another, as I have loved you.

It is easy to do evil things,
easy to harm oneself.
To do what is good,
what is good for oneself,
is very difficult.

No branch can bear fruit, by itself,
unless it remains on the vine.
So you can bear no fruit, unless you remain
in me.

If a man becomes what he asks others to become,
then he can teach them truly.
But the self-control needed for this is truly difficult.

Come to me, all you who struggle and are
weary, and I will give you rest.

The self must be master of the self. Who else can be
the master? When the self is conquered a master is
hard to find.

Do not let yourself be called "rabbi."
You have one rabbi, and you are all brothers.
Do not let yourself be called "father."
You have one Father and he is in heaven.
Do not let yourself be called "teacher."
You have one Teacher, the Messiah.

Whoever abandons the envy of others
is serene, by night and by day.

Who are you to say to God, "Why did you
make me thus?"
Is he not free to make two vessels out of
the same lump of clay, one a treasure, and
one for common use?

The man who has cut the strap, the thong, the
rope, all that ties, the man who raises the beam
which closes the door, who is awake - - - I call him
a Brahmin.

Whoever loves father and mother more than
me is not worthy of me.
Whoever loves son or daughter more than
me is not worthy of me.

The man for whom there is neither this shore
nor the other shore nor both shores, the man
who is free and unbound, he is a Brahmin.

Foxes have their dens and birds their
roosts; the Son of Man has nowhere to lay
his head.

I call the man a Brahmin whose future is
not known to gods or spirits or men, whose
ways are pure, who has become a saint.

The wind blows where it wills; you hear the
sound of it but know not where it comes
from or where it is going. So it is with
everyone born of the spirit.

He is a Brahmin who is free of desire, who has no
doubts because he knows, who has reached the
Immortal.

> Anyone who sets his hand to the plow and
> then looks back is not fit for the Kingdom of
> God.

Cross the stream with diligence, Brahmin,
leaving your desires. When you understand
the passing away of all that is, you will know
what does not perish.

> If anyone wishes to be my follower, let
> him leave self behind, take up his cross
> day after day, and come after me.

A Brahmin is like the moon:
pure, serene, and full of peace.

> In me you will find peace.

He is a Brahmin who knows his past lives,
who has seen heaven and hell, who will not
be born again, who is full of knowledge, who
has become perfect.

> If you dwell in my words you will indeed
> be my disciples, you will know the truth,
> and the truth shall set you free.

Empty the boat: emptied it will move quickly.
Leave behind passion and hate, and sail to Nirvana.

> If you will be perfect, sell what you have
> and give it to the poor. Then come, follow
> me.

Abandon what is before, abandon what is behind,
abandon what is in the middle. Cross to the other shore.
If your mind is free you will not return to the way of
death.

Unless you become like little children,
you cannot enter the Kingdom of Heaven.

Leave anger and pride, leave everything that ties.
No suffering can harm the man who owns nothing.

How happy are the poor in spirit,
theirs is the Kingdom of Heaven.

What we are comes from what we have thought, it
is made up of our thoughts. If a man speaks or acts
with evil thoughts in his heart, suffering follows him
as surely as the wheel follows the beast that pulls
the wagon.

The body's lamp is the eye.
If your eye is clear, your body will be full
of light.
If your eye is clouded, your body will be
full of darkness.

A man who sees and dwells upon the sins of others
allows his own sins to grow, and he is far from
leaving them.

You are so intent on taking the speck of
dust out of your brother's eye that you fail
to notice the plank in your own.

A wise man who listens to the teachings becomes
clear and peaceful, like a lake.

His mother treasured all these things in her
heart.

Buddha said: Subhuti, all those who strive for compassion should think thus: all living creatures of

110

whatever kind have been liberated by me. Yet when
all of these have been liberated, no being has been
liberated. Why, Subhuti? Because no one who is truly
compassionate cherishes the thought of ego, personality, being, or individuality.

> Greater things than these will you do,
> for I go to the Father.

Subhuti asked the Buddha: Will there always be
people who come to believe after hearing the teachings?
Buddha answered: There will always be those who
respond to the teachings with pure faith. They will
not cherish ego, personality, being, or individuality.
Nore will they cherish non-ego, impersonality,
unbeing, or non-individuality. To do so would be to
cherish ego, personality, being, and individuality. You
must not be attached to any of these things. This is
why I compare my teaching to a raft. Even this teaching must be left behind – and how much more so false
teaching!

> When the Son of Man returns, will he find any
> faith on the earth?

> Leave all you have, and follow me.

Subhuti, could one say that the Buddha is enlightened?
Does he have a teaching to communicate? Subhuti
answered: As I understand it, one cannot say that the
Buddha is enlightened or that he has a teaching to
communicate. Why? Because the Buddha has said
that truth cannot be contained; it is inexpressible. It
neither is nor is not.

> If you cannot understand when I talk to you
> about the things of earth, how will you under-
> stand when I talk about the things of heaven?

111

Subhuti, does the free man say to himself, "I shall have the reward of one who is not reborn?" No, because these are merely words. There is no such condition as "not being reborn." The one who knows this is not reborn. Subhuti, does the holy man say to himself, "I have reached enlightenment"? No, because there is no such thing as "enlightenment."

> I am not concerned about my own glory.
> There is one who does care, and He is judge.

Subhuti, a compassionate man should not think to himself, "I will liberate all living beings." He should not think in terms of separate beings. He is truly compassionate when he lays this thought aside.

> Let not your left hand know what your right hand is doing.

Then Subhuti asked the Buddha: When you reached enlightenment, did you gain anything? Not a thing, Buddha answered. That is why it is called the final and perfect enlightenment.

> He emptied himself,
> taking the form of a slave,
> becoming like unto men.